POEMS OF PEACE

Including the
Lyrical Dramatic Poem
Eolaus

by

JAMES ALLEN

With an Essay from
Within You is the Power

by

HENRY THOMAS HAMBLIN

First published in 1907

British Library Cataloguing-in-Publication Data
A catalogue record for this book is available
from the British Library

CONTENTS

3

THE USE OF
THE SPIRITUAL OR
SUPER-CONSCIOUS MIND.

An Excerpt From *Within You Is The Power*
By Henry Thomas Hamblin

We have already seen that the sub-conscious mind, wonderful though it be, is instinctive merely, lacking inspiration and what we call originality. All inspiration comes from the Universal Mind, via the super-conscious. All poets and inspired writers get their inspiration in this way.

This higher mind is not recognized by Psychologists, but it has long been known to searchers for spiritual truth.

What we get from the sub-conscious is the outcome of facts and knowledge supplied to it. What we get from the super-conscious is direct inspiration from higher planes. This higher mind might also be called the Mind of Illumination, for those who can enter into it become illumined, being able to know the Truth and to see things as they really are, and not as they falsely appear to the senses.

This limited consciousness in which we live is bounded by our five senses. The universe that we see around us is partly real and partly an illusion. The real universe is Spiritual and infinite: what we sense is a limited, partial conception of a fragment of it. Our limited, finite conception of the universe is entirely misleading and erroneous, and so long as we rely on sense evidence and the human mind, we remain in darkness and uncertainty. When, however, we can rise into the super-conscious realm, our consciousness expands, transcending the senses and the limitations of the physical plane.

The Spiritual mind is, of course, only accessible to those who are more delicately attuned to its finer vibrations. Nothing that is worth having can be had without effort, and it is only after much self-discipline that it becomes possible for the student to raise his consciousness to this higher realm and understand life from the standpoint of the Universal Mind.

There is nothing, either mystical or psychical, about the use of this higher mind. One who makes use of it becomes spiritually-minded, that is all. He does not go into trances, nor need he become clairvoyant: he simply remains a sane, normal individual, with this difference only—he makes use of more of his mind than does the ordinary individual.

One who is able to use this higher mind develops that which has been termed "the divine quality of originality." If ever a person is to rise above the dead level of mediocrity it must be through direct inspiration from higher planes, through his super-conscious mind. If ever a person is to bring forth a new idea which shall enrich humanity and add to the common good, it must come through the higher mind.

One who is properly attuned, becomes, through the super-conscious mind, a recipient of knowledge that is above human, and wisdom that is divine. He knows by direct knowing: he becomes wise through an influx of Divine Wisdom. He is able to distinguish between the real and the sham, between the gold and the dross: he is also able to see and recognize the right path in life—a thing utterly impossible to the mind of the senses—and to tread it, thus being led into the only true success and real good of which his life is capable. Let it be said here that all Wisdom must come from within. While books and the written word may be helpful, it is the Spirit within the reader that illumines the word, and makes it real and true to the seeker after Wisdom. One who realizes that he is illumined within by the Divine Spirit, and that this alone can bring him into real knowledge is well advanced on the path that leads to realization.

The wisdom of the human mind always leads to disappointment. It is based on the evidence of the senses, which is erroneous, therefore its findings must always be lacking in real wisdom. One who relies upon the inspiration of Divine Wisdom has often to decide to take a course of action which, apparently, is opposed to his best interests. Yet, if he follows the inward Wisdom, he finds that he is always guided aright, and, later, has cause to be devoutly thankful that he followed the gleam.

EOLAUS

A LYRICAL DRAMATIC POEM

DRAMATIS PERSONAE

Eolaus.
The Prophet.
Earth.
Heaven.
Cosmos.
Voices of Nature.
Voices of Truth.
Echoes.

SCENE

A beautiful Island, wooded.
Eolaus sitting on a fallen tree near the sea-shore.

EOLAUS.
Unto this lonely Island I repair
To search for peace. After long, days and nights
Upon the waters, storm-tossed and fatigued,
My skiff Touched thy fair harbour, blessed Isle.
Now on thy fragrant bosom I will rest,
And in thy spiritual ecstasy
Sweetly participate : thy loveliness

Entrances me; thy restfulness enweaves
My thoughts with peace imperishable ; thou
Art silent, solitary, beautiful,
And I am lonely ; yet thy solitude
Perchance will comfort me, and take away
My loneliness and pain. O Solitude !
Thou habitation of aspiring hearts ;
Thou light and beacon of the pure ; thou guide
Of them that cry in darkness ; thou sweet friend
Of sorrow stricken wanderers; thou staff
And stay of the strong climber up the hills,
Trackless and strange, of Truth; instructor thou,
And teacher of the teachable and true,
Beloved of the lowly, wise and good,
Be my companion now, and take away
The world's ache from my bosom! I am tired
Of the vain Highways, where the noise and din
Drowns all but sad remembrance ; tired of all
The tumult and the terror and the tears
That rule discordant in the House of Life,
Shaking but not destroying, as the storms,
Confederate with the oceans, shake the shores
And rock-bo'und margins of the continents.
I seek the peace that does not change ; the calm
That knows no storm ; the Silence that remains.
Pleasure disturbs, and does not satisfy :
When the excitements of the senses fade,
Sorrow and pain return, and leave the heart
Remorseful, desolate. As o'er the waste
And barren moor the lonely curlew cries.
So wails the bird of anguish o'er the mind
Sated with pleasure; Woe and Want repair
To the abode of Selfishness, and take
Legions of miseries with them. I would find
Where Wisdom is, where Peace abides, where Truth,

Majestic, Changeless, and eternal, stands
Untouched by the illusions of the world:
For surely there is Knowledge, Truth, and Peace
For him who seeks, seeing that ignorance
And error and affliction are; these prove
The unseen truths obversely: darkness makes
Light sure and certain, though we see it not.
We sleep and wake, and, waking, know the dream
That troubled us in sleep ; how it arose,
Phantasmal and chaotic, in the mind
Left all ungoverned ; even so perchance
This life of passion and of wild desire
(Troubled, chaotic, and not understood),
May be, as 'twere, a dream ; and if a dream
Of the unmastered mind, we shall awake
Out of the nightmare of our miseries,
And know the gladness of Reality.
But how shall one awake ? How, if not by
Bridling his passions, curbing his desires
By masterful dominion of the will ?
If passions be the troubled dreams of life,
And not its substance and reality,
Then he who shakes off passion shall awake
And know the Truth ; surely this must be so !
Therefore unto this unfrequented place
Have I addressed myself, that I may gain,
By purity and strong self-mastery,
Th' awakened vision that doth set men free
From painful slumber and the night of grief.
Here unobserved and solitary, I
Will purify my heart and train my mind
In the true ways of sweet unselfishness,
Subduing self and passion ; so perchance
The changeless Truth will be revealed to me,
And I shall move, wherever Duty calls,

11

Serene and sorrowless.

Moreover, here
An aged Prophet dwells, so I am told,
Who will instruct me in the Silent Way
Which winds through the morasses of the mind
Unto the firm heights of accomplished Truth.
Him will I seek when I have slept awhile,
For weariness now urges me to rest.

Lies down.

Thou Zephyrus! thou sweet and cooling breath
That tempercst the broiling mid-day rays
Of June's extremest heat, blow o'er me now,
And fan me into sweet forgetfulness !
I am a-wearied, battling with the waves.
Now will I sleep : after my long, long search
Upon the waters, I am spent with toil.
Watch o'er me. Nature, I am safe with thee.

Sleeps.

VOICES OF NATURE.

FIRST VOICE.

Listen, O Eolaus !

Woven of passion is the Universe;
Vain is thy puny strength to break its web.
Submit thyself to that which in thee cries ;
Gratify nature; do not fly delight.

Eolaus, come !
Let me lead thee, Eolaus!

Let me guide thee, Eolaus!

Come, Eolaus! Eolaus, come!

ECHO.
>   Eolaus, come !

SECOND VOICE.
>   There is sweet intoxication
>   In the Pleasure - house of Earth ;
>   Aye - renewed exhilaration,
>   Love and happiness and mirth.

FIRST VOICE.
>   Come, Eolaus! Eolaus, come !

ECHO.
>   Eolaus, come !

THIRD VOICE.
>   What is seen is sure ;
>   What is felt is known
>   Pleasure is secure;
>   Joy is life alone.

FIRST VOICE.
>   Come, Eolaus ! Eolaus, come!

ECHO.
>   Eolaus, come!

SECOND VOICE.
>   Come and drink the wine of life ;
>   Pleasure's vintage come and taste ;
>   Leave thy fruitless search and strife;

Holy vigils wear and waste
Youth, for love and revels framed:
Nature thus is blindly blamed.

FIRST VOICE.

Come, Eolaus ! Eolaus, come !

ECHO.

Eolaus, come !

THIRD VOICE.

Think no more of low and high ;
Leave thy climbings, and forget
Aim and struggle, doubt and sigh ;
Level is the pathway set
Of enjoyment: seek no more ;
Rest thou here, thy woe is o'er

FIRST VOICE.

Eolaus come!
Let me lead thee, Eolaus !
Let me guide thee, Eolaus !

Come, Eolaus! Eolaus, come!

ECHO.

Eolaus, come !

EARTH.

Unnumbered ages have I rolled
Through the abysmal spaces ;And eons new from eons old
Th' Eternal Finger traces ;And I must follow where it
moves ;
No rest ! no rest!
With hopes and fears and hates and loves

14

Unblest ! unblest!

FOURTH VOICE.

Listen, O Eolaus !

Sorrow doth darken all the universe ;
Its creatures are involved in pain and woe ;
Helpless they cry, and no one hears or aids ;
Dark, dark is life, and none its meaning know.

Eolaus, hear !
None can lead thee, Eolaus !
None can guide thee, Eolaus !

Hear, Eolaus! Eolaus, hear!

ECHO.
Eolaus, hear!

FIFTH VOICE.
There is pain and woe and sorrow
In the hospital of Earth ;
Every night and morn and morrow
Bringeth drought and death and dearth.

FOURTH VOICE.
Hear, Eolaus ! Eolaus, hear !

ECHO.
Eolaus, hear!

SIXTH VOICE.
What is Sean's unsure;
What is felt is blown;

15

Self is insecure;
Life is pain alone.

FOURTH VOICE.

Hear, Eolaus ! Eolaus, hear !

ECHO.

Eolaus, hear !

SEVERAL VOICES.

We moan and sigh ;
We sob and cry ;
We wander, like the wind upon the stream,
Vainly for peace,
Seeking release
From the keen pain of our unending dream.

FOURTH VOICE.

Eolaus, hear!
None can lead thee, Eolaus !
one can guide thee, Eolaus !
Hear, Eolaus ! Eolaus, hear!

ECHO.

Eolaus, hear!

VOICES OF TRUTH.

FIRST VOICE.

Awake, O Eolaus!
Arise ! Shake off the dreams of Night,
Open thine eyes, and sec the Light;
Passionless Wisdom waits for thee
In sorrowless serenity.
Leave thou the fleeting shapes of Time,

The rugged Way of Truth sublime
Walk thou ; nor fear, nor grieve, nor lust,
Scorning the self whose end is dust.
Wake, Eolaus! Eolaus, wake !

CHORUS OF VOICES.
Eolaus, wake!

SECOND VOICE.
Knowledge is for him who seeks ;
Wisdom crowneth him who strives;
Peace in sinless silence speaks;
All things perish, Truth survives

FIRST VOICE.
Wake, Eolaus ! Eolaus, wake !

VOICES.
Eolaus, wake!

THIRD VOICE.
Follow where Virtue leads,
High and still higher;
Listen when Pureness pleads,
Quench not her fire.
Lo ! he shall see
Reality,
Who cometh upward, cleansed from all desire.

FIRST VOICE.
Wake, Eolaus ! Eolaus, wake !

VOICES.
Eolaus, wake!

FOURTH VOICE.

    He who attaineth unto Purity
    The faultless Parthenon of Truth doth see.
    Awake! disperse the dreams of self and sin !
    Behold the Shining Gateway ! enter in!

FIRST VOICE.

    Wake, Eolaus ! Eolaus, wake !

VOICES.

    Eolaus, wake !

FIFTH VOICE.

    Conquer thyself,
    Then thou shalt know;
    Climb to the high,
    Leave thou the low.
    Deliverance
    Shall him entrance
    Who strives with sins and sorrows, tears and pains
    Till he attains.

FIRST VOICE.

    Wake, Eolaus ! Eolaus, wake !

VOICES.

    Eolaus, wake!

HEAVEN.

    In the visions of the ages
    I am evermore reflected ;
    In the precepts of the Sages
    I am spoken and rejected.

I can suffer no distortion,
Sin and sorrow cannot stain me ;
Fixed and faultless in proportion,
He must bend who would attain me.

EOLAUS, WAKING.
Who will lead me, who will guide me
In my deep perplexity?

HEAVEN.
In the middle of the Island
Waits the sage whom you are seeking;
On the Rock which cannot crumble
Sits the Prophet who will guide you.

Eolaus wakes.

EOLAUS.
'Mid the conflicting visions of the mind
I darkly grope, and nevermore can find
The steadfastness and surety that I seek ;
Where clamour reigns the Silence connot speak;
So many voices and so many ways !
So many wand'rings the nights and days!
One way I seek, one voice I long to hear,
But Truth eludes me and does not appear,
Now to this Island's centre I repair
To seek the Prophet who abideth there.

The scene changes to the centre of the Island. An aged and venerable man appears, sitting upon a rock.

EOLAUS.
Art thou the Prophet whom I seek ?

PROPHET.
 I am.

EOLAUS.
 Be thou my guide, for thou art wise, and I
 Am ignorant; speak thou, and I will hear;
 Teach me, and I will be instructed ; make
 Me to behold the Path which leads to Truth,
 And I will walk if though it be o'erstrewn
 With flints and burrs; and if it needs must come
 Within the round of holy discipline
 That one shall walk that way with naked feet,
 Or else forego the end and view of Truth,
 Then barefoot I will walk it, and account
 Bleedings and wounds and lacerations
 As aids unto my will and fortitude,
 As tasks wisely ordained, and so to be
 Gladly encountered in my pilgrimage.
 Mine ears are open, open thou mine eyes,
 For I am blind, and cannot find my way.

PROPHET.
 He who would see with the all-seeing eye
 Single of Truth, must first his blindness know.
 He cannot see who does not wish to see,
 Thinking he sees already, while his acts
 Proclaim his spiritual blindness. Truth
 Waits on the Lowly - hearted. He who knows
 That being passion - bound, he yet is blind,
 Has groped his way to Wisdom. Thou dost see.

EOLAUS.

    I see naught but the darkness of my mind,
    And in that darkness ever - changing shapes
    Of things phantasmal that perplex and haunt,
    Eluding knowledge ; I am ignorant,
    Yet strive to know ; nor will I cease to strive
    Till I attain.

PROPHET.

    Seeing thy darkness, thou
    So far dost see ; knowing thine ignorance,
    So far hast thou attained to knowledge : seek,
    And thou shalt surely find.

EOLAUS.

    How shall I seek ?

PROPHET.

    Increase thy strength and self-reliance; make
    The spectres of thy mind obey thy will :
    See thou command thyself; nor let no mood,
    No subtle passion nor so swift desire
    Hurl thee to baseness; but, should'st thou be hurled,
    Rise and regain thy manhood, taking gain
    Of lowliness and wisdom from thy fall.
    Strive ever for the mastery of thy mind,
    And glean some good from every circumstance
    That shall confront thee; make thy store of strength
    Richer for ills encountered and o'ercome.
    Submit to naught but nobleness; rejoice
    Like a strong athlete straining for the prize,
    When thy full strength is tried; be not the slave
    Of lusts and cravings and indulgences,

Of disappointments, miseries and griefs,
Fears, doubts, and lamentations, but control
Thyself with calmness; master that in thee :
Which masters others, and which heretofore
Has mastered thee: let not thy passions rule,
But rule thy passions; subjugate thyself
Till passion is transmuted into peace,
And wisdom crown thee; so shalt thou attain
And, by attaining, know.

EOLAUS.

    Hard is the path.
Which thou hast set before me; steep and strange
Its ascent; unfamiliar and unknown
The Place whereto it leads: I see it rise
Precipitous but yet accessible,
Beyond the reach of vision: what awaits
The climber, none but he who climbs may know;
For if one ask, and, with believing ears
Attend the spiritual Mountaineer
In his depicture of the unknown heights,
What knows he more, though more believing ? What
Gains he but words, and wonderings, and dreams,
Unless he also climb ? I would o'ermount
Faith, and ascend to knowledge; I would not
Rest idly in the valleys of belief,
Content with speculation ; I would be
The Mountaineer, and know.

PROPHET.

    The Mountaineer
Is he who, dauntless, climbs.

EOLAUS.

 But yet the way,—
 Where leads it ? All beyond the reach of sight
 Is dark, unknown, mysterious. What avails
 The strenuous ascent, if some precipice
 The daring climber claim, or loosened rock
 Dash him to death, or cold and hunger make
 Ravage upon his strength ? Passion is sweet,
 And 'tis enjoyed and known; and round about
 The habitations at the mountain's base,
 In the familiar valleys of the mind,
 Twine the sweet flowers of soft affections,
 Filling the air with fragrance and delight,
 And mellow fruits of love and labour hang
 Ripe for the plucking; shall I these renounce,
 The sure and known, for the unsure, unknown ?
 Are these not safe, substantial and possessed ?
 While that I seek,—Where is it ? Is this Truth,
 This idea of Reality which haunts
 My mind, and drives me whither I know not,
 Itself a speculation ? What abides ?
 Alas! all that we have and know is caught
 In transiency; changes that never end
 Roll wave - like o'er the restless universe
 .And man is tossed therein; so it befalls
 That everything which comes into his grasp—
 Bearing the face of an enduring joy—
 After a little fever of delightIs torn away again: nothing
 endures :
 All things are dying even while they live;
 And life is passing while it seems to wait.
 There is no sweet possession, no rare joy,
 No cherished circumstance, no prized delight

No lovely thing, of which it can be said,—
"There is no time when this will never be."
What comes to pass, passes, and conies no more;
What grows, decays; what rises, falls; what lives
And flourishes, dies and doth fade away:
Where then is surety; Where is knowledge? Where
Is rest and refuge?

PROPHET.
    There is rest in Truth.

EOLAUS.
    Is there no rest in death ?

PROPHET.
    There is no rest
    In death.

EOLAUS.
    No rest in death nor life ?

PROPHET.
    No rest
    In death nor life; yet or in death or life,
    Where Truth is, there is rest.

EOLAUS.
    Prophet of Good
    Lead me to the Abiding; set my feet
    Upon the austere Highway which doth lead
    To the Eternal City ; I would find
    The rest and refuge of undying Truth.

PROPHET.

    Look thou within. Lo, in the midst of change
    Abides the Changeless; at the heart of strife
    The Perfect Peace reposes. At the root
    Of all the restless striving of the world
    Is passion, and at passion's heart is stored
    Truth; yea, the Law of laws is in thy mind,
    And written on the tablet of thy heart
    Are its eternal edicts: subjugate
    Thy passions, and the truth will be revealed,
    For whoso follows passion findeth pain,
    But whoso conquers passion findeth peace.

EOLAUS.

    Not to be subject unto passion, but
    To subject passion,—is this then the way ?

PROPHET.

    Thou hast well said. As the sweet nut is held.
    In the hard shell, and cannot be enjoyed
    But by destruction of the husk, so Truth
    In passsion is preserved, but is not known
    Till passion be destroyed and cast away.
    He who preserveth passion, dreading loss
    Of sweetness and enjoyment, cannot know
    The bliss of Truth, nor find where wisdom is:
    He is a prodigal, feeding upon
    The husks of life, the empty shows of things.
    And knowing not its kernel, seeing not
    The changeless substance of Reality.
    He only knows who conquers evil; he,
    Who masters self, passes beyond the dim
    Uncertain light of faith, and on him breaks

The light of Perfect Knowledge which enfolds
Emancipation, gladness, perfect peace.

EOLAUS.

I know that sorrow follows passion; know
That grief and emptiness and heartaches wait
Upon all earthly joys ; so am I sad ;
Yet Truth must be, and, being, can be found;
And though I am in sorrow, this I know—
I shall be glad when I have found the Truth.

PROPHET.

There is no gladness like the joy of Truth.
The pure in heart swim in a sea of bliss
That evermore nor sorrow knows, nor pain ;
For who can see the Cosmos and be sad ?
To know is to be happy; they rejoice
Who have attained Perfection; these are they
Who live, and know, and realize the Truth.

EOLAUS.

I strive for that Perfection; shall I reach
The Heights of Blessed Vision ?

PROPHET.

Comfort ye,
The Heights of Blessed Vision ye shall reach.

EOLAUS.

Yet how, and when, and where ? I am confused.
The Way is near, and yet I see it not!

PROPHET.

He must be friendly with the worm and toad
Who would be the companion of the wise,

And know the Cosmic Splendour; he must stoop
Who seeks to stand; must fall who fain would rise ;
Must know the low, ascending to the high :
He who would know the Great, must not disdain
To diligently wait upon the small:
He wisdom finds who finds humility.

EOLAUS.
Speak on, O Prophet! I attend thy words,

PROPHET.
The beasts can neither bend nor stand erect
Being beasts,—abandon bestial tendencies;
But man can bend, and man can stand erect,
Being man,— embrace pure thoughts and stainless deeds ;
Here is deliverance. Man's redemption lies
In man himself, yet is not born of self,
But takes its rise in Truth: man can achieve
He findeth Truth who findeth self-control.

EOLAUS.
When I have found the meaning of thy
words,I know I shall be wise as thou art wise ;
But now I hear thee, and yet hear thee not.

PROPHET.
Thou wilt perceive the substance of my words,
And understand their meaning, when they stir
That meaning in thyself, and in thy mind
Stand clear and well-reflected; thou canst know
Only by subjugation of thyself,
And practice of the highest: all that's real
Is inward; outward things are fleeting shows,
Vain and illusory, holding nor rest
Nor refuge for the wise : obey the Right,

And wrong shall ne'er again assail thy peace,
Nor error hurt thee more: attune thy heart
To Purity, and thou shalt reach the Place
Where sorrow is not, and all evil ends.
The Holy Ones know not the name of sin ;
Goodness and Truth make glad the good and true :
The Perfect Ones behold the Perfect Law;
Struggle and strife are ended in the Truth.
All things are holy to the holy mind,
All uses are legitimate and pure,
All occupations blest arid sanctified,
And every day a Sabbath.

EOLAUS.

    I perceive
Some glimmering of a Light transcending light,
Some outline of a mighty Principle
More beautiful than beauty; see some dim
Appearing of the vision of a Life
Vaster than life : the Cosmos is sublime !
My eyes will open, I shall see the Truth,
And, seeing, shall be glad for evermore !

PROPHET.

    Be mindful, or the thought that soars will sink :
Be lowly, patient, well-instructed; hold
Thyself in check-, by many single steps
All journeys reach completion: as the tree
That rears its stately head toward the sky—
Bestowing shade and shelter—issued from
A tiny seed, and, waiting patiently
Upon the law of growth, it came to be
The thing majestic that it now appears,—
So wisdom from a single act of good
Well-planted, watched, and watered, comes at last

To its sublime proportions.

EOLAUS.

    I will tend
    The plant of wisdom with all diligence,
    And watch its growth toward perfection.
    Show me the unobserved and lowly Way ;
    Let praise, reward, and popularity
    Be no more sweet to me, and no more sought;
    Let self be blotted out, I seek the Truth.

PROPHET.

    Now listen, and attend:—the pigeons pick
    Holes in the buildings, and the storm o'erturns
    That they had weakened: little failings eat
    Holes in the citadel of Character
    Which, weakened thus, cannot withstand the storms
    Of circumstance, but weakly falls before
    Tempestuous temptations. As the bee
    Buildeth the honeycomb, the bird its nest,
    The builder his strong house, e'en bit by bit,
    Straw unto straw, and stone laid upon stone,
    Until the finished thing and perfect whole
    Crowns effort with success,—so the wise man.
    By adding thought to thought and deed to deed
    In ways of good, buildeth his character.
    Little by little he accomplishes
    His noble ends; in quiet patience works
    Diligently, while others sleep, or slake
    Their hot desires in riot; nowise moved
    From his main purpose by perplexities,
    Falls, errors, failures, difficulties, pains,
    Daily he builds into his heart and mind
    Pure thoughts, high aspirations, selfless deeds,
    Until at last the edifice of Truth

Is finished, and behold! there rises and appears
The Temple of Perfection.

EOLAUS.

I have found
The little Gate mean and moss-grown which leads
Into a dark, despised, neglected Way
Which, further, leads to glorious esplanades
And heights of Splendour; foolish men avoid
The lowly, and thereby the lofty lose;
Despise the small, and the majestical
Miss, and see not. Prophet of Good and Truth,
Wisely and well hast thou instructed me ;
Thou hast revealed to me the Path of Peace ;
My eyes are opened, and at last I see
Thy lowly Way, and I will enter in.

PROPHET.

The Perfect Way awaits thy strenuous tread ;
Behold where rise, precipitous, yet grand,
The Hills of Virtue ; higher, and beyond,
The Peaks of Blessedness ; and yet again,
Upon the lofty Summits of the Truth,
Where clouds and darkness are not, and where rests
Eternal Splendour; there, abiding Joy
Awaits thy coming. Onward, and disperse
The dark delusions of thy self! Evil
Is Good denied, is darkness and no more.
Let self be nothing, and the Truth be all ;
Thus conquer pain: acquire serenity;
Wisdom accompanies tranquillity;
The self-subdued the fadeless Glory know :
Be watchful, fearless, faithful, patient, pure :
By earnest meditation sound'the depths
Profound of life, and scale the heights sublime

Of Love and Wisdom. He who does not find
The Way of Meditation, cannot reach
Emancipation and enlightenment.
But thou wilt find the Way of Holy Thought;
With mind made calm and steadfast, thou wilt see
The Permanent amid the mutable,
The Truth eternal in the things that change :
Thou wilt behold the Perfect Law: Cosmos
From Chaos rises when the conquered self
Lies underneath man's heel: Love be thy strength;
Look on the passion-tortured multitudes,
And have compassion on them ; know their pain
By thy long sorrow ended. Thou wilt come
To perfect peace, and so wilt bless the world,
Leading unto the High and Holy Way
The feet of them that seek.—And now I go
To my Abode; go thou unto thy work.

EOLAUS.

Prophet of Peace, I go: and unto Thee,
Spirit of Truth, I come. To all the world,
And all that lives, for evermore be peace.

COSMOS.

I am; Perfection is, and Peace ;
Evil is gone, beholding Me ;
And they from sin and sorrow cease
Who look upon my Symmetry.
When fault and failure find my Form,
Lo, fault and failure are no more !
I am the sunshine and the storm,
The whisper, and the ocean's roar !
The creeping action that deceives,
The lie, the theft, the murderer's ire,
All these my Crucible receive,

31

They burn in my Celestial Fire.
All superstitions, errors, wiles,
The crawling craft, the cruel lust,
All that debases and defiles
I grind, and scatter in in the dust.
The Nations rise, the Empires fall,
And I eternally rehearse,
To scene and strain majestical,
The Drama of the Universe.
The Eons pass, the systems pale,
Unchanged their changes behold ;
They listen, and I tell my Tale;
I all their fleeting forms enfold.
Who knoweth Me, becometh Me;
Who hath my Vision finds release
From Darkness and Captivity.
I am ; Perfection is, and Peace.

MISCELLANEOUS POEMS

BUDDHA

Under Mount Ratnagira's western shade,
Weary and worn with his long search for Truth,
Sorrowing, unsatisfied, disconsolate,
Sat Buddha, knowing not where he should turn
To find the Truth that he had so long sought—
The Truth that maketh steadfast, strong, and pure,
The Truth that bringeth peace and blessed rest.
The Schools had failed him; the philosophies,
Hoary and ancient, had not stilled the cry
Of passion in his heart; and passion's child,
Sorrow, was with him still; the scriptures, creeds,
Proud pillars of the State, had failed to bear
The weight of his great woe, crumbling away
Under temptation, leaving him the prey
Still of desire and pain and clouded mind.
Mortifications he had tried, and they
Had left him strengthless, wan, wanting the Truth;
And now he seemed as one defeated, borne
Upon the stream of Fate, helpless, alone.

But while the Buddha brooded in the shade,
Suddenly on his ear there fell a cry,

A sob of pain, a pitiful strange sigh ;
Whereat he rose, and left the shade, and sought
(He scarce knew why, but that there leaped within
His sorrowing heart a mighty unknown love)
Whence came the cry; and presently he saw,
Upon the road, 'mid thirsty clouds of dust,
Under the fierce blaze of the Indian sun,
A shepherd, driving hard a flock of sheep;
And in the rear there lagged a little lamb
With wounded feet, bleating most piteously,
The while the ewe, with anguish deep and sore,
Cried o'er her little one, knowing that she
Was helpless to relieve her.

When Buddha saw
The piteous spectacle, compassion slew
His own deep sorrow; and he straightway took
The wounded Iamb, and bore it in his arms,
Saying, 'Vain are the strivings of the soul
After vain knowledge; vain the learned lore
That hath not pity in it; vain is life
That hath not love; and whatsoe'er is false,
And what uncertain, though it seemeth true,
This thing is true, that I should pity thee.
The priests who pray and read, and read and pray,
Die in their sins at last, and do not find
The Love I mourn for, the deep Truth I seek ;
And better where it that I ease thy pain
Than pray with them, and seek and never find.
Thee will I love; yea, I will pity thee
Whom none will pity; thee will I relieve ;
Tired of the soulless theories of men,
I, Buddh, will stoop to thee, thou dumb, weak thing,
Whom men despise, knowing that this is true,
Whate'er is doubtful, and whate'er unsure,

Pity and Love are right; what ever fades
And perishes, Compassion will not fade,
And Love will never perish." So he took
Into his arms the weary, wounded thing
Which nestled in his bosom, and became
Quiet and peaceful; and the anxious ewe
Walked by his side, looking into his face,
Glad that her lamb had found those blessed arms :
And so she walked, and dumbly worshipped him,
Knowing him Buddha, the compassionate.

And Buddha in that hour entered the Way
Which he had vainly sought in schools and creeds;
Entered the Path which no philosophy
Leads unto, and which none shall ever find
But by sweet deeds of Love, forgetting self;
And in his heart there grew a holy Love ;
And in his mind a knowledge new and strange ;
And his whole being felt a painless peace ;
Sorrow and pain were not ; and then he knew
hat he had found the holy Truth at last.

And from thenceforward Buddha lived the Truth,
And taught its practice; and from far and near
Came men and women who had sought the Truth,
And at his feet they sat and worshipped him,
Learning of love and pity ; finding bliss
And peace that cannot fail; and him they called
Deliverer, Redeemer, Blessed Lord.
And even they who understood not, sensed
Faintly this truth which one day they should know :—
Better than learning is a loving heart;
And to give comfort to one wounded lamb
Is higher than the wisdom of the schools,
And greater than the world's philosophy.

IF MEN ONLY UNDERSTOOD

If men only understood
That the wrong act of a Brother
Should not call from them another,
But should be annulled with kindness,
That *their* eyes should aid his blindness,
They would find the Heavenly Portal
Leading on to Love immortal—
If they only understood.

If men only understood
That *their* wrong can never smother
The wrong-doing of another ;
That by hatred hate increases,
And by Good all evil ceases,
They would cleanse their hearts and actions.
Banish thence all vile detractions—
If they only understood.

If men only understood
That the heart that sins *must* sorrow,
That the hateful mind to-morrow
Reaps its barren harvest, weeping,
Starving, resting not, nor sleeping;
Tenderness would fill their being.
They would see with Pity's seeing—
If they only understood.

If men only understood
All the emptiness and aching
Of the sleeping mid the waking
Of the souls they judge so blindly,
Of the hearts they pierce unkindly.
They, with gentler words and feeling,
Would apply the balm of healing—
If they only understood.

If men only understood
That their hatred and resentment
Slays their peace and sweet contentment
Hurts themselves, helps not another,
Does not cheer one lonely Brother,
They would seek the better doing
Of good deeds which leaves no rueing-—
If they only understood.

If men only understood
How Love conquers ; how prevailing
Is its might, grim hate assailing;
How Compassion endeth sorrow,
Maketh wise, and doth not borrow
Pain of passion; they would ever
Live in Love, in hatred never—
If they only understood.

PRACTICE AND PERCEPTION

———————————

Questioning Life and Destiny and Truth,
I sought the dark and labyrinthine Sphinx,
Who spake to me this strange and wondrous thing :—
" Concealment only lies in blinded eyes,
And God alone can see the Form of God."

I sought to solve this hidden mystery
Vainly by paths of blindness and of pain,
But when I found the Way of Love and Peace,
Concealment ceased, and I was blind no more :
Then saw I God e'en with the eyes of God.

LIBERTY

———————————

The unwise say, " Our sufferings are unjust,
Our pains and woes rise from the scattered dust
Of sinful ancestors ; we are not free ;
Our fathers robbed us of our liberty
By what they did ; and we are weak and frail
Because they erred; they fell, and we must fail.

" Our drunkenness comes from their love of wine ;
Our lusts their revels made ; and we divine
Our manifold diseases by the ways
In which they walked; and as they trod the maze
Made by their feet, so we must likewise tread,
For we are bound and driven by the dead."

Thy sins are thine, O man ! and from thy deeds
Thy life, with all its weal and woe, proceeds ;
By self, and not by others, thou art bound ;
In thine own will and heart the root is found
Of all thy lack of peace; ope thou thine eyes,
Leave the dead past, and look within ; be wise.

Make pure thy heart, and thou wilt make thy life
Rich, sweet, and beautiful, unmarred by strife ;
Guard well thy mind, and, noble, strong, and free,
Nothing shall harm, disturb or conquer thee ;
For all thy foes are in thy heart and mind ;
There also thy salvation thou wilt find.

Mind is the Master-power that moulds and makes.
And Man is Mind and evermore he takes
The Tool of Thought, and, shaping what he wills,
Brings forth a thousand joys, a thousand ills :—
He thinks in secret, and it comes to pass ;
Environment is but his looking-glass.

In his own heart he fosters dark desires,
Or strives for good, or loftily aspires ;
In his own life he reaps what he has sown,
Or pain or peace, he garners in his own.
Thou man, that bowest to heredity,
Know this—the Law of life is Liberty,

By Thought we rise ; by Thought we fall ; by Thought
We stand or go: all destiny is wrought
By its swift potency; and he who stands
Master of Thought, and his desires commands,
Willing and weaving thoughts of Love and Might,
Shapes his high end in Truth's unerring Light.

LONG I SOUGHT THEE

Long I sought thee, Spirit holy,
 Master Spirit, meek and lowly;
Sought thee with a silent sorrow, brooding o'er the
     woes of men ;
 Vainly sought thy yoke of meekness
 'Neath the weight of woe and weakness;
Finding not, yet in my failing, seeking o'er and o'er again.

 In unrest and doubt and sadness
 Dwelt I, yet I knew thy Gladness
Waited somewhere ; somewhere greeted torn and
     sorrowing hearts like mine ;
 Knew that somehow I should find thee,
 Leaving sin and woe behind me,
And at last thy Love would bid me enter into Rest divine.

 Hatred, mockery, and reviling
 Scorched my seeking soul, defiling
That which should have been thy Temple, wherein thou
     should'st move and dwell ;

Praying, striving, hoping, calling ;
Suffering, sorrowing in my falling,
Still I sought thee, groping blindly in the gloomy
    depths of hell.

And I sought thee till I found thee;
And the dark Powers all around me
Fled and left me silent, peaceful, brooding o'er thy
    holy themes ;
 From within me and without me
 Fled they when I ceased to doubt thee ;
And I found thee in thy Glory, mighty Master of
    my dreams !

Yea, I found thee, Spirit holy,
Beautiful and pure and lowly;
Found thy Joy and Peace and Gladness ; found thee in
    thy House of Rest;
 Found thy strength in Love and Meekness,
 And my pain and woe and weakness
Left me, and I walked the Pathway trodden only by
    the blest.

REALITY

I see men gaze upon the distant skies
 Of ideals inaccessible and vain;
And miss the Holy Way which near them lies—
 The hourly conquest over sin and pain.

41

I see uplifted and imploring hands
 Aching with emptiness; I see the cause,
Self-made, of man's long sorrow; see his bands
 Self-wrought, self-bound; I see the broken laws.

Wisdom lies hidden in our common life,
 And he will find it who shall rightly ask ;
Where springs the fretful fever and the strife
 There Truth abides—e'en in the daily task.

Behold where Love Eternal rests concealed !
 (The deathless Love that seemed so far away!)
E'en in the lowly heart; it stands revealed
 To him who lives the sinless life to-day.

Wrapped in our nearest duty is the Key
 Which shall unlock for us the Heavenly Gate ;
Unveiled, the Heavenly Vision he shall sec,
 Who cometh not too early nor too late.

The glory of the Truth no Future veils
 From tear - stained eyes; no Past obliterates,
For toil - worn feet, the narrow, weed - grown trails
 Which wind through common ways to joyful Gates.

Where'er we go immortal splendour goes ;
 But eyes, self-blinded, look and cannot see ;
Th' Eternal Glory shines upon man's woes,
 Piercing the dark night of his misery.

Lo ! where the shadowless Effulgence gleams—
 In tasks well done, in stainless thoughts and deeds,
In words of love and pity, not in dreams
 Of sky - bound glories holding future meeds.

Peace cometh only to the peaceful soul;
 Love, painless, nestles in the Love-born heart ;
Joy springs where self is sunken for the whole;
 From conquered sins immortal beauties start.

Our task is with us, and the Path Sublime,
 Rising from swamps of self, through Duty's way,
Cuts its clear course up the steep hills of Time
 Unto the splendour of the Perfect Day.

TO-MORROW AND TO-DAY

In the dark land of To-morrow
 I dwelt with pain and sorrow,
And I sighed for joys and blessings that escaped me as
   I ran ;
 And the darkness gathered round me,
 For the morrow ever found me
Living in "What I ought to do," and not in *what I can.*

And I sought for loving-kindness
 In the dim, dark haunts of blindness ;
In the lightless caves of self I searched for blessedness
   and rest;
 And I reached out hands appealing,
 Sadly groped for light and healing,
Striving for " what I want to have, " not *what is true
   and best.*

Then I found that selfish hoping,
 Darkly seeking, blindly groping
In vain wishing and regretting chased life's glory
        frommy brow;
 So I ceased from selfish fretting,
 Turned to Love, and, self-forgetting,
Left " what I hope to get and keep," for *what I will be now.*

So I fled from self and sorrow,
 Left the dark land of To-morrow,
And thought of what kind deeds to do, what loving
        words to say;
 And the light of peace and gladness
 Chased away the clouds of sadness,
For I lost the past and future in the bright world of To-day.

STAR OF WISDOM

Star that of the birth of Vishnu,
Birth of Krishna, Buddha, Jesus,
Told the wise ones, Heavenward looking,
Waiting, watching for thy gleaming.
In the darkness of the night-time.
In the starless gloom of midnight;
Shining Herald of the coming
Of the kingdom of the righteous:
Teller of the mystic story
Of the lowly birth of Godhead
In the stable of the passions,

44

In the manger of the mind-soul ;
Silent singer of the secret
Of compassion deep and holy
To the heart with sorrow burdened,
To the soul with waiting weary:—
Star of all-surpassing brightness,
Thou again dost deck the midnight ;
Thou again dost cheer the wise ones
Watching in the creedal darkness,
Weary of the endless battle
With the grinding blades of error ;
Tired of lifeless, useless idols,
Of the dead forms of religions ;
Spent with watching for thy shining ;
Thou hast ended their despairing;
Thou hast lighted up their pathway ;
Thou hast brought again the old Truths
To the hearts of all thy Watchers ;
To the souls of them that love thee
Thou dust speak of Joy and Gladness,
Of the Peace that endeth sorrow.
Blessed are they that can see thee,
Weary wanderers in the Night-time ;
Blessed they who feel the throbbing,
In their bosoms feel the pulsing
Of a deep Love stirred within them
By the great power of thy shining.
Let us learn thy lesson truly ;
Learn it faithfully and humbly;
Learn it meekly, wisely, gladly,
Ancient star of holy Vishnu,
Light of Krishna, Buddha, Jesus.

WOULD YOU SCALE
THE HIGHEST HEAVEN

Would you scale the highest heaven,
 Would you pierce the lowest hell,—
Live in dreams of constant beauty,
 Or in basest thinkings dwell.

For your thoughts are heaven above you,
 And your thoughts are hell below ;
Bliss is not, except in thinking,
 Torment naught but thought can know.

Worlds would vanish but for thinking ;
 Glory is not but in dreams ;
And the Drama of the ages
 From the Thought Eternal streams.

Dignity and shame and sorrow,
 Pain and anguish, love and hate
Are but maskings of the mighty
 Pulsing Thought that governs Fate.

As the colours of the rainbow
 Make the one uncoloured beam,
So the universal changes
 Make the One Eternal Dream.

And the Dream is all within you,
 And the Dreamer waileth long

For the Morning to awake him
To the living thought and strong.

That shall make the ideal real,
 Make to vanish dreams of hell
In the highest, holiest heaven
 Where the pure and perfect dwell.

Evil is the thought that thinks it ;
 Good, the thought that makes it so ;
Light and darkness, sin and pureness
 Likewise out of thinking grow.

Dwell in thought upon the Grandest,
 And the Grandest you shall see;
Fix your mind upon the Highest,
 And the Highest you shall be.

TO THEM THAT SEEK
THE HIGHEST GOOD

To them that seek the highest Good
 All things subserve the wisest ends;
 Naught comes as ill, and wisdom lends
Wings to all shapes of evil brood.

The darkening sorrow veils a Star
 That waits to shine with gladsome light;

Hell waits on heaven; and after night
Comes golden glory from afar.

Defeats are steps by which we climb
 With purer aim to nobler ends;
 Loss leads to gain, and joy attends
True footsteps up the hills of time.

Pain lead to paths of holy bliss,
 To thoughts and words and deeds divine ;
 And clouds that gloom and rays that shine,
Along life's upward highway kiss.

Misfortune does but cloud the way
 Whose end and summit in the sky
 Of bright success, sunkiss'd and high,
Awaits our seeking and our stay.

The heavy pall of doubts and fears
 That clouds the Valley of our hopes,
 The shades with which the spirit copes,
The bitter harvesting of tears,

The heartaches, miseries, and griefs,
 The bruisings born of broken ties,
 All these are steps by which we rise
To living ways of sound beliefs.

Love, pitying, watchful, runs to meet
 The Pilgrim from the Land of Fate ;
 All glory and all good await
The coming of obedient feet.

ONE THING LACKING

E'en at the Master's holy feet, low kneeling,
 Came one who knew nor wordly want nor stress
Yet sad with fruitless search for Truth, and feeling
 Perchance the Teacher of the world might bless
Then asked he softly, and with humble pleading,—
 "Good Master, canst Thou calm my inward strife?
Show me the lofty highway of Thy leading ;
 What shall I do to gain Eternal Life?"

Then He, the Lord of Life, looked down in kindness
 Upon the Kneeling form, and, answering, said,—
"Thou knowest the commandments, be not mindless
 Of these, and thou shalt live, though thou wert dead."
Replied the Kneeling one,—"All these things keeping
 From my youth up, I sought Thee out this day,
Yet still I wander unawakened, sleeping;
 I have not found the high and holy Way."

Yet lackest thou one thing, yield thy desiring,"
 (Thus spake the Master), "do not grasp, but give;
Sell that thou holdest, and, with free aspiring,
 Come, follow Me, and thou shalt truly live;
For whoso follows Me, all selfish clinging
 Yielding with pure and undivided mind
Shall nothing lack; yea, for his earthly bringing
 Surely the Heavenly Treasure he shall find."

Now he who knelt was very rich, and cherished
  His earthly treasure in his inmost heart;
And even there his spirit paused and perished,
  Losing renunciation's better part:
Noble but not complete, the Master leaving
  To cleave unto his perishable day,
He chose the path of passing things and grieving,
  And, sorrow-stricken, went his lonely way.

YASHAS

Lo, in the night, when all the world was sleeping,
  Yashas, the noble and aspiring youth,
Pondering upon the world's great sorrow, weeping,
  Searched for the holy pathway unto Truth.
" I search in vain," said he, " and will betake me
  Unto the Blessed One, and seek release ;
Healer of sorrow, he perchance will make me
  Partaker in his deep, Nirvanic peace."

Then came the youth, with footsteps fast and faster,
  Unto the Blessed Teacher of mankind,
And, weeping, fell before the Holy Master,
  Saying, "Great Lord, I seek and cannot find.
How great is my distress and tribulation !
  Thou knowest all my sorrow and my pain ;
Give me the holy balm of thy salvation,
  Let me depart not from thy side again."

The Blessed One, seeing his perturbation,
  Spake softly thus unto the gentle youth
" Lo, here is no distress, no tabulation ;
  Come unto Me, and I will show you Truth
The Truth will bring you joy, dispelling sadness,
  And as the night before the light of day
Flees and departs, e'en so your rising gladness
  Sorrow and pain and care will chase away."

Then spake He of things pure and high and holy
  Giving full freely of His wisdom's store,
And Yashas, listening, rapt, all meek and 'lowly
  Drank deeply of the Master's wondrous lore ;
And lo! the cooling breath of Wisdom o'er him
  Stole softly, fanning all his care to rest ;
Sorrow departed, and Compassion bore him
  Unto the Path the Master's feet had prest.

THE LOWLY WAY

All ways are waiting for my feet to tread,
The light and dark, the living and the dead,
The broad and narrow way, the high and low,
The good and bad, and with quick step or slow,
I now may enter any way I will,
And find, by walking, which is good, which ill.

And all good things my wand'ring feet await,
If I but come, with vow inviolate,

51

Unto the narrow, high and holy way
Of heart-born purity, and therein stay ;
Walking, secure from him who taunts and scorns,
To flowery meads, across the path of thorns.

And I may stand where health, success, and power
Await my coming, if, each fleeting hour,
I cling to love and patience: and abide
With stainlessness; and never step aside
From high integrity ; so shall I see
At last the land of immortality.

And I may seek and find; I may achieve ;
I may not claim, but, losing, may retrieve,
The Law bends not for me, but I must bend
Unto the Law, if I would reach the end
Of my afflictions, if I would restore
My soul to Light and Life and weep no more.

Not mine the arrogant and selfish claim
To all good things; be mine the lowly aim
To seek and find, to know and comprehend,
And wisdom-ward all holy footsteps wend
Nothing is mine to claim or to command,
But all is mine to know and understand.

THE MUSIC OF THE SEA

I love to hear the music of the sea,
  As, playing on the everlasting shore,
Its strange, profound, and mystic melody,
  It chants the soul of man for evermore.

It sings of wreckful passion when it beats
  With unrestrained wildness on the rocks;
Then with succeeding sorrow it retreats,
  Sobbing o'er pain of self- inflicted shocks.

Of martyrdom and silent pain it speaks
  When, dumbly moaning, languidly it rolls ;
And weirdly wails, as on the rocks it breaks,
  The deadness and despair of human souls.

Its scintillations on the pebbly beach,
  Mingling with sunshine and the playful breeze,
Are bubbling merriment and mirth that reach
  No deeper than the sensuous vision sees.

When, scarcely murmuring, placidly it lies,
  It whispers of the silent heart of peace;
Of that unutterable state where dies
  Passion, and all our human sorrows cease.

Playful, perturbed, peaceful, tempestuous,
  Reflected in thy heart, thy peace, thy strife,

Is the strange passion and peace in us,
　The madness and the wisdom of our life.

Thou symbol of the human soul, O sea!
　I love to hear thee, on the lonely shore
Chanting thy everlasting melody,
　Singing the soul of man for evermore.

LOVE'S CONQUEST

I stood upon the shore, and saw the rocks
　Resist the onslaught of the mighty sea,
And when I thought how all the countless shocks
　They had withstood through an eternity,
I said, " To wear away this solid main
The ceaseless efforts of the waves are vain."

But when I thought how they the rocks had rent,
　And saw the sand and shingles at my feet
(Poor passive remnants of resistance spent)
　Tumbled and tossed where they the waters meet,
Then saw I ancient landmarks' neath the waves,
And knew the waters held the stones their slaves.

I saw the mighty work the waters wrought
　By patient softness and unceasing flow ;
How they the proudest promontory brought
　Unto their feet, and massy hills laid low ;

How the soft drops the adamantine wall
Conquered at last, and brought it to its fall.

And then I knew that hard, resisting sin
 Should yield at last to Love's soft ceaseless roll
Coming and going, ever flowing in
 Upon the proud rocks of the human soul;
That all resistance should be spent and past,
And every heart yield unto it at last.

TO MY DAUGHTER NORA
ON HER TENTH BIRTHDAY

Since when thou earnest, with thy native charms,
A weeping infant to thy mother's arms,
Ten fleeting years have lifted up thy head
Unto my breast ; ten years of love are fled,
But all their store of innocence and bliss
Remains with thee; thy mother's and my kiss
Seal it for ever thine! Those guileless ways
Which, walking, have filled up thy tender days,
May'st thou for ever keep; may thy pure heart
Keep always pure, that no unholy dart
Pierce it with anguish; may remorse and pain
Shrink from thy hallowed presence, and no stain
Soil thy white robes of peace. O ! be thou sure
Bliss follows in the footsteps of the pure.
And whatsoe'er shall tempt of wrong or strife,
Hold fast the rare gem of a blameless life ;

Nor lose, nor lightly hold, but bind to thee
The priceless jewel of thy purity.

THE INWARD PURITY

Find ye that life is anguish, and that self-love is a chain
That binds thy quivering soul, and cuts with biting
    stings of pain?
Grieve ye where Slander's serpents trail beneath fair
    flowers of Trust ?
Or weep where Friendship buried lies 'neath Hatred's
    fulsome dust?
Then listen,—Selfish sweets are brief, and fleeting
    self-hood's ties,
But there abides a fadeless Love, a Life that never dies;
A path there is which Serpent slime hath never yet defiled,
Where weary feet find rest and peace, and are no more
    beguiled:
And that pure Love and Life are his whose inmostheart
    is free.
From unforgiveness, judgment false, and self and enmity ;
And that fair Path of Peace he walks whose memory holds
    no stain
Of injuries past; that blameless heart hath reached the end
    of pain.

SELF-SACRIFICE

Great glory crowns the heights of hope by arduous
    struggle won;
Bright honour rounds the hoary head that mighty works
    hath done ;
Fair riches come to him who strives in ways of
    golden gain,
And fame enshrines his name who works with genius-
    glowing brain:
But greater glory waits for him who, in the bloodless strife
'Gainst self and wrong, adopts, in love, the sacrificial life;
And brighter honour rounds the brow of him who, 'mid
    the scorns
Of blind idolaters of self, accepts the crown of thorns ;
And fairer, purer riches come to him greatly strives
To walk in ways of love and truth to sweeten human lives ;
And he who serveth well mankind exchanges fleeting
    fame
For Light eternal, Joy and Peace, and robes of heavenly
    flame.

I TAKE REFUGE IN TRUTH

I come to thee, O Master! on thy breast
 I lay my weary head; I lave thy feet
With tears and kisses, travail of my quest;
 I bring my aching heart and sore defeat,
And seek thy holy joy and perfect rest.

Place thou thy hand upon my burning brow;
 Soothe thou my soul, and bid my sins depart;
I ask thy sweet salvation even now ;
 Thy rest I seek to ease my throbbing heart;
Thou art the Truth, to thee I cling and bow.

Thou changest not amid Earth's changing scenes;
 All worldly joys, strong passions that decay,
The sordid thought, the action that demeans,
 These are not thee, and they will pass away :
On thy abiding strength my spirit leans.

Lead thou my feet unto thy Holy Place ;
 I take thy chastening; thy great love I sec ;
Thy rod I kiss, and in my deep disgrace,
 With longing, humble heart I cling to thee,
Knowing thou wilt not turn away thy face.

I, TRUTH, AM THY REDEEMER

I, Truth, am thy Redeemer, come to Me;
 Lay down thy sin and pain wild unrest;
And I will calm thy spirit's stormy sea,
 Pouring the oil of peace upon thy breast:
Friendless and lone—lo, I abide with thee.

Defeated and deserted, cast away ;
 What refuge hast thou? Whither canst thou fly?
Upon My changeless breast thy burdens lay;
 I am thy certain refuge, even I:
All things are passing ; I alone can stay.

Lo I, the Great Forsaken, am the Friend
 Of the forsaken; I, whom men despise,
The weak, the helpless, and despised defend ;
 I gladden aching hearts and weeping eyes:
Rest thou in Me, I am thy sorrow's end.

Lovers and friends and wealth, pleasures and fame—
 These fail and change, and pass into decay ;
But my Love does not change ; and in thy blame
 I blame thee not, nor turn My face away :
In My calm bosom hide thy sin and shame.

THE WHITE ROBE

The White Robe of the Heart Invisible
 Is stained with sin and sorrow, grief and pain,
And all repentant pools and springs of prayer
 Shall not avail to wash it white again.

While in the path of ignorance I walk,
 The stains of error will not cease to cling;
Defilements mark the crooked path of self,
 Where anguish lurks and disappointments sting.

Knowledge and wisdom only can avail
 To purify and make my garment clean,
For therein lie love's waters; therein rests
 Peace undisturbed, eternal, and serene.

Sin and repentance is the path of pain,
 Knowledge and wisdom is the path of Peace ;
By the near way of practice I will find

 Where bliss begins, how pains and sorrows cease.

Self shall depart, and Truth shall take its place ;
 The Changeless One, the Indivisible
Shall take up His abode in me, and cleanse
 The white Robe of the Heart Invisible.

THE RIGHTEOUS MAN

No harmful shaft can reach the righteous man,
 Standing erect amid the storms of hate,
Defying hurt and injury and ban,
 Surrounded by the trembling slaves of Fate.

Majestic in the strength of silent power,
 Serene he stands, nor changes not nor turns ;
Patient and firm in suffering's darkest hour,
 Time bends to him, and death and doom he spurns.

Wrath's lurid lightnings round about him play,
 And hell's deep thunders roll about his head ;
Yet heeds he not, for him they cannot slay
 Who stands whence earth and time and space are fled.

Sheltered by deathless love, what fear hath he?
 Armoured in changeless Truth, what can he know
Of loss and gain? Knowing eternity,
 He moves not whilst the shadows come and go.

Call him immortal, call him Truth and Light
 And splendour of prophetic majesty
Who bideth thus amid the powers of Night,
 Clothed with the glory of divinity.

CHOICE

The will to evil and the will to Good
Are both within thee: which wilt thou employ?
Thou knowest what is right and what is wrong;
Which wilt thou love and foster? which destroy?

Thou art the chooser of thy thoughts and deeds;
Thou art the maker of thine inward state ;
The power is thine to be what thou wilt be;
Thou buildest Truth and Love, or lies and hate.

If thou dost choose the evil, loving self,
Thy cries and prayers for Good shall all be vain;
Thy thought and act bringeth thee good or ill ;
Deep in thy heart thou makest joy and pain.

As thou pursuest Good, striving to make
Evil depart, thou shalt rejoice and say,—
" Lo! Light and Love and Peace attend on me;
Truth fadeth not, and Good abounds away."

Choose as thou wilt thy thoughts and words and deeds,
And as thou choosest so shall be thy life;
The will to Good shall bring thee Joy and Peace,
The will to evil, wretchedness and strife.

TRUTH TRIUMPHANT

There is no height to which thou canst not climb;
  There is no grandeur that thou may'st not view,
If thou wilt reach beyond the things of Time,
  Unto the Pure, the Beautiful, the True.

There is no saintly vision, no glad sight
  Of seer, nor no dream of holy sage
But may be thine ; nay, is thy heavenly right,
  If thou wilt claim thy regal appanage.

There is no sin but thou may'st overthrow;
  There is no vileness that, octopus-like,
Binds thee its victim, but thou soon canst know
  The way and weapon thy strong foe to strike.

Thou art not framed for sin and grief and shame;
  Thou art not bent to grovel in the mire;
But thou art made erect, and given a name,
  Hast hands to reach, and spirit to aspire.

Glory and strength and triumph — these are thine;
  Rise up, and conquer every inward foe ;
Behold the heavens, how radiantly they shine !
  Stand up and strike, O conqueror of woe!

O THOU WHO WOULD'ST TEACH!

_____

O thou who would'st teach men of Truth!
 Hast thou passed through the desert of doubt?
Art thou purged by the fires of sorrow? hath ruth
 The fiends of opinion cast out
Of thy human heart ? Is thy soul so fair
That no false thought can ever harbour there ?

O thou who would'st teach men of Love !
 Hast thou passed through the place of despair ?
Hast thou wept through the dark night of grief? does it
move
 (Now freed from its sorrow and care)
Thy human heart to pitying gentleness,
Looking on wrong, and hate, and ceaseless stress ?

O thou who would'st teach men of Peace!
 Hast thou crossed the wide ocean of strife?
Hast thou found on the Shores of the Silence, release
 From all the wild unrest of life?
From thy human heart hath all striving gone,
Leaving but Truth, and Love, and Peace alone?

IF THOU WOULD'ST
RIGHT THE WORLD

If thou would'st right theworld,
And banish all its evils and its woes,
  Make its wild places bloom,
And its drear deserts blossom as the rose,—
  Then right thyself.

If thou would'st turn the world
From its long, lone captivity in sin,
  Restore all broken hearts,
Slay grief, and let sweet consolation in, —
  Turn thou thyself.

It thou would'st cure the world
Of its long sickness, end its grief and pain,
  Bring in all-healing Joy,
And give to the afflicted rest again,—
  Then cure thyself.

If thou would'st wake the world
Out of its dream of death and dark'ning strife,
  Bring it to Love and Peace,
And Light and brightness of immortal Life,—
  Wake thou thyself.

WHAT OF THE NIGHT?

What of the night, O Watchman ! see'st thou yet
 The glimmering dawn upon the mountain heights
 The golden Herald of the Light of lights,
Are his fair feet upon the hilltops set ?

Cometh he yet to chase away the gloom,
 And with it all the demons of the Night?
 Strike yet his darting rays upon thy sight?
Hear'st thou his voice, the sound of error's doom?

The Morning cometh, lover of the Light;
 E'en now He gilds with gold the mountain's brow,
 Dimly I see the path whereon e'en now
His shining feet are set toward the Night.

Darkness shall pass away, and all the things
 That love the darkness, and that hate the Light
 Shall disappear for ever with the Night:
Rejoice! for thus the speeding Herald sings.

KNOWLEDGE

We find the Good by being good, the True
 By being true, the Real by dissolving
Our fond illusions, thereby piercing through
 Shadow, and knowing substance. By resolving,
We can attain, and by attaining, know ;
 And, knowing, who shall cause us grief or harm?
What trembling victim of the world's vain show
 Shall pierce the armoured heart, or foil the arm
Of him whose Shield is Wisdom? What event,
 What circumstance, what mutability
Can shake the Changeless? And whoso hath blent
 His life with Changeless Good, stands steadfastly
In Knowledge, fearing nothing, hating naught;
His heart and mind Love-fashioned, Wisdom-wrought.

THE END OF EVIL

All evil passes from us when we find
The Way of Good ; when word and deed and mind
Are shaped to Truth and Wisdom; then we see
The end of bondage and captivity.

All good is ever with us ; we but want
Wisdom to take it; we are poor and scant
Only in lacking wisdom ; that acquired,
The good is ours that we so long desired.

Be stilt any soul and know that peace is thine;
Be steadfast, heart, and know that strength divine
Belongs to thee : cease from thy turmoil, mind,
And thou the Everlasting Rest shalt find.

MAN DIVINE

Man is superior to sin and shame,
 Evil and error he will yet dethrone,
The beasts within he will o'ercome and tame,
 The brute will pass, the Angel wtll be known ;
Yea, even now the Man divine appears,
Crowned with conquest, victor o'er all fears.

Hail to thee, Man divine ! the conqueror
 Of sin and shame and sorrow; no more weak,
Wormlike and grovelling art thou ; no, nor
 Wilt thou again bow down to things that wreak
Scourgings and death upon thee; thou dost rise
Triumphant in thy strength ; good, pure, and wise.

PATIENCE

Why this fierce struggle to achieve thine ends ?
This selfish argument ? This fire which lends
  Heat to resentment, ashes to remorse?
Canst thou bend Truth and Nature to thy will ?
Bend thou, and work and wait; be strong and still ;
  Soft growth is stronger than vehement force.

Be as a flower, content to be, to grow
In sweetness day by day; content to know
  The hidden blessing in the seeming curse ;
A child of Love, unargumentative;
Content to be and know — as thou dost live—
  The simple secret of the Universe.

RESTORED

Eager for strife and struggle, Self and gain,
  And heeding not the gentle Voice of Truth,
We strive and wrestle in dark ways of pain,
And, blind and lost in passion, we disdain
  The unobtrusive Way of Love and ruth ;

So live we on in sorrow and in woe,
Nor rest can find, nor blessed gladness know.

Tired of strife and anger, hate and pain,
 And weary of the wranglings of the Schools,
We turn, and look into your face again,
Beloved brother, sister; nor in vain
 Search we with purer eyes; but as in pools
Soft, deep, and silent, gaze we, finding rest;
So pass we on our way, refreshed and blest.

ON RELEASING A CAPTIVE BIRD

I found a little bird held fast, ensnared
 By ruthless hands; a gentle, captive prey
Thirsting for freedom, piteously scared,
 Struggling in vain to 'scape and soar away.

I marked his terror, and I took him up ;
 His fluttering heart spoke out his wild despair.
"Look, you and I with the great gods shall sup
 This day," I said ; then threw him into air.

Whereat he soared, and wheeled, and flew away;
 Great was his joy, and ruth - born bliss was mine ;
Thus supped we both with the high gods that day ;
 Thus tasted we their nectar, drank their wine.

ART THOU IN SORROW?

Art thou in sorrow? Art thou in despair,
  Involved in doubt and deep perplexity?
Leave thou thyself, and with thy fellows share
  The good thou hast, and thou wilt blessed be.

Let Love's bright sunshine play upon your heart;
  Come now unto your gladness, peace, and rest ;
Bid the dark shades of selfishness depart,
  And now and evermore be truly blest.

WHEN I AM PURE

When I am pure
I shall have solved the mystery of life,
  I shall be sure,
When I am free from hatred, lust, and strife,
I am in Truth, and Truth abides in me.
I shall be safe and sane and wholly free
  When I am pure.

IMMORTALITY

He shall not die who seeks the Way of Truth ;
He shall not see the corruption who doth walk
With stainless feet the Path of Purity ;
He shall not wander in dark worlds of woe
Who finds the Gate of Good and enters there,
For he shall taste of immortality
While feasting at the table of his Lord.

ARE YOU SEARCHING?

Are you searching for the happiness that does not
    fade away?
Are you looking for the joy that lives, and leaves no
    grievous day?
Are you panting for the waterbrooks of Love, and Life,
    and Peace?
Then let all dark desires depart, and selfish seeking cease.

Are you ling'ring in the paths of pain, grief-haunted,
    stricken sore ?
Are you wand'ring in the ways that wound your weary
    feet the more ?

Are you sighing for the Resting-Place where tears and
    sorrows cease ?
Then sacrifice the heart of self, and find the Heart of Peace

www.ingramcontent.com/pod-product-compliance
Lightning Source LLC
Chambersburg PA
CBHW030135260626
47156CB00008B/2952